written by
Solveig Paulson Russell
illustrated by
Robert A. Jones

A is for Apple, and WHY*

*THE STORY OF OUR ALPHABET

ABINGDON PRESS

New York   Nashville

To my daughter, Brenda, who has always been fascinated with letters and what they have to say

Thousands and thousands of years ago, there was a time when no one knew how to write. In those days most people lived in caves. There were no towns, no cities, and no schools of any kind.

Children learned to fish and to hunt. They learned to make axes and other things of stone. They learned to make simple clothes of animal skins. But they did not learn to read or write. They learned all of the things they needed to know from the people around them.

Children long ago watched other people to find out how to do things. And they listened when their mothers and fathers told stories of things that had happened long before. The mothers and fathers had heard the stories many years earlier from their mothers and fathers.

Then one day someone drew a picture on the wall of a cave. No one today knows when this happened, who drew the picture, or even what the picture showed. But it was probably a picture of some kind of animal. And it was probably drawn more than 50,000 years ago.

Other people saw this first picture and began to draw pictures on the walls of their caves. The pictures were of animals they had seen and hunted.

The first pictures that people drew were all
of animals standing still. But after a while
this changed. New pictures showed animals
running, fighting, or eating, and some of
them showed people. A group of pictures together told a story.

Stories told with story-telling pictures
were the first stories ever written down.
These stories did not have to be told aloud to
be remembered.

The pictures were drawn on the walls of
caves with charcoal. Coloring materials were
made from plants. Wood or bone tools were

used for brushes or pens to put on the color.

Children, sitting on the cave floors, may also have drawn pictures. They may have watched their fathers and then made lines with their fingers in the dirt floor of the cave. They probably drew pictures of animals, just as their fathers did.

At first people who made picture-story drawings all lived in caves. But after thousands of years some of them learned to live in tents or in houses made of sticks or clay. Then they drew pictures on the walls of their houses. Pictures were also made on clay bowls and plates, on tools, and on jewelry.

Tools of stone or of metal were used to make the drawings. Colored sand and clay, as well as plant colorings, were then used for paints.

It took a long time to make a good picture-story drawing. So artists began to make their pictures more simple. Instead of finished pictures, they drew signs or symbols to stand for pictures. Some of these symbols looked like "stick figures."

Picture symbols are called *pictograms*.

In the beginning each artist made up his own pictograms. Only people who knew what his pictograms stood for could read what he had written.

Then people who lived near each other started to use the same pictograms. Some people now lived in villages and even in cities. And sometimes one city came to rule a great deal of land, and it became a country. When this happened, people all over the country used the same pictograms.

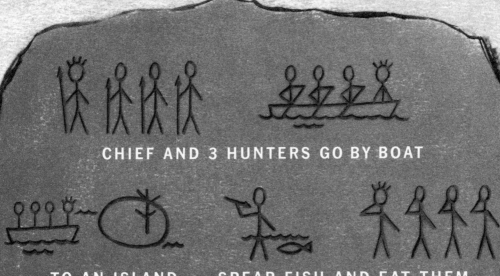

CHIEF AND 3 HUNTERS GO BY BOAT

TO AN ISLAND . . . SPEAR FISH AND EAT THEM

FIRST DAY . . TAKE BOAT TO LAND . . GO INTO MOUNTAIN

HUNTERS CATCH A DEER . . . SECOND DAY

HUNTERS RETURN HOME . . . THIRD DAY

Egypt was one of the first countries to use the same pictogram writing everywhere. The symbols the Egyptians used are called *hieroglyphics*.

At first the Egyptian hieroglyphics were just like the pictograms used in other places. Each pictogram was a picture of the thing it stood for, and once people understood what each picture stood for, the writing could be read.

The picture below shows some of the early Egyptian pictograms.

The Egyptians wrote only with pictograms for a long time. But there were many messages people could not write with them. There were no symbols to stand for *a week* or *courage* or *strength* or *wisdom*. These are ideas, not things, and they cannot be seen. Because ideas cannot be seen, early artists had not made picture symbols for them.

But the Egyptians wanted to write about ideas. And they finally solved their problem by making pictures or symbols of parts of things that seemed to suggest ideas. These pictures are called *ideograms*.

Six thousand years ago all Egyptian hieroglyphics were made up of pictograms and ideograms.

Not all children went to school in those days. Many children had to go to work when they were very young. But those children who did go to school had to learn thousands and thousands of hieroglyphic symbols before they could read and write.

Each symbol these children learned stood for a different thing or idea. It stood for the thing or idea itself. It did not stand for the words that people spoke when they talked about things or ideas. People today hardly need to speak Egyptian to read early Egyptian hieroglyphics. They need only know the meaning of each symbol to read any such piece of writing.

In the Egyptian language some words sounded alike but did not mean the same thing. We have words like this, too: *flour* and *flower*, and *two* and *to*, for example.

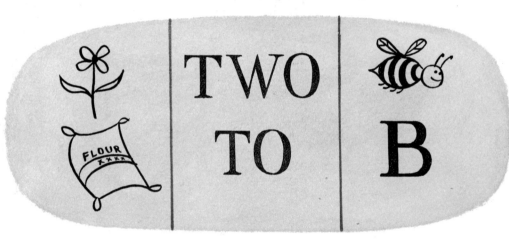

Because people could not remember all of the thousands of ideograms and pictograms, they began to use the same symbol for different things and ideas when the words for them sounded alike. This meant that symbols began to stand for words, as well as for things and ideas themselves.

Symbols that stand for words are called *phonograms*. To read the Egyptian phonograms, people must know the Egyptian language. Phonograms were used with pictograms and ideograms.

One phonogram stood for one word. But sometimes two or more phonograms were combined to write one long word.

Because phonograms for short words could be combined to make long words, fewer symbols were needed in writing. This made reading and writing easier.

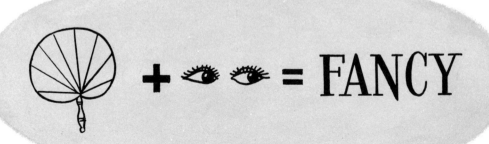

After many years, some Egyptian symbols came to stand for sounds that were not words at all. These sounds were like the ones we make when we say *au* or *fa* or *ing*. Such sounds are called syllables. They are made up of one or more sounds that are spoken together as a single part of a word. A symbol that stands for a syllable is called a *syllabary*. Several syllabaries are needed to write one word.

The Egyptian children who learned syllabaries found that they were hard to read. They were written one after another. There was no way to tell when one word ended and another began. And there was no way to tell when one sentence ended and another began. To make the meaning clear, pictograms, ideograms, and phonograms were used, too.

After the Egyptians had used syllabaries for many years, some hieroglyphics came to stand for only one sound. Symbols that stand for one sound are called *letters.*

The Egyptians finally had twenty-four letters. All of the letters stood for sounds that we call *consonants.* The consonants we use are *bcdfghjklmnpqrstvwxyz.* The Egyptians had no letters for the sounds we call *vowels, aeiou.*

The twenty-four Egyptian letters almost made an *alphabet.* An alphabet is a group of letters that can be used to read and write all of the words of a language. But without vowel letters, Egyptian writing was hard to read. Pictograms, ideograms, phonograms, and syllabaries had to be used, too. So the letters did not make an alphabet.

People in Egypt often needed to send messages from one part of the country to another. Such messages were written on papyrus, a kind of paper made from reeds that grew in swampy places. Ink and brushes or pens made of reeds or quills were used for writing.

Curved lines were the easiest lines to make with pens or brushes, so gradually the hieroglyphic symbols came to have more and more curves when they were written on papyrus. Finally each symbol was joined to the next with a line so that the writing looked very much like our handwriting. This writing was called *hieratic* writing. It was used only on papyrus for business letters and stories. The hieroglyphic symbols were still carved on stone buildings.

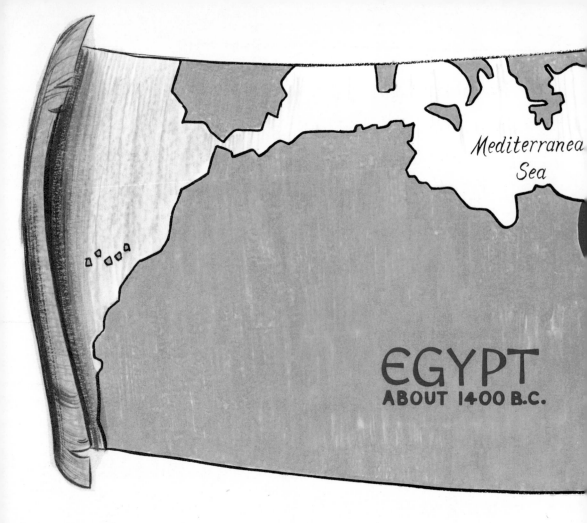

Egyptian hieroglyphics and hieratic writing were used in many places. But other people in other countries had other ways of writing things down.

The Sumerians, Assyrians, Babylonians,

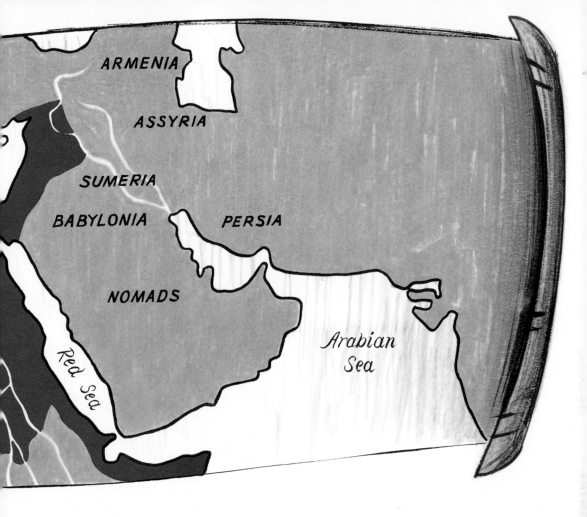

Persians, and others who lived east of the Egyptians could write. Their writing had pictograms, ideograms, syllabaries, and even some letters. But it looked quite different from the Egyptian writing.

The near eastern people wrote on clay tablets shaped like bricks. They used a sharp tool called a stylus to write with. Symbols were made in wet clay, and then the clay was baked hard to make the symbols last as long as the tablet lasted.

The easiest kind of mark to make with the stylus was a wedge-shaped mark. So all of the symbols were made up of straight lines and wedge-shaped marks. This is called *cuneiform* writing.

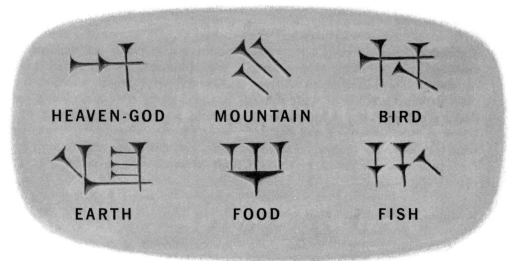

HEAVEN-GOD   MOUNTAIN   BIRD

EARTH   FOOD   FISH

Living near the people who used cuneiform writing were people called the Phoenicians. They lived on the Mediterranan Sea and sailed in small boats to other countries where they could trade and sell their goods. They needed a simple way to write so they could keep track of the things they bought and sold.

Because they traveled to many countries, the Phoenicians knew cuneiform writing and they also knew the Egyptian ways of writing. But all of these, even hieratic writing, took too long to learn and too long to write.

The Egyptian letter symbols, however, were easy to learn. So the Phoenicians took the idea of letters from the Egyptians. They borrowed shapes for their letters from Egyptian and cuneiform writing. And finally they had a group of twenty-two letters that they could use.

Children who learned to write in those days in Phoenicia did not have to learn thousands of symbols. They had only twenty-two letters to learn. Every word in their language could be written with those twenty-two letters. The letters made up the first true alphabet.

Phoenician children learned to write from right to left. And they wrote only capital letters. There were no small letters. There were no spaces between words to show where one word ended and the next word began. And there were no periods at the ends of sentences.

The letters in the Phoenician alphabet were all consonants just as the Egyptian letters were. There were no vowel letters. But the Phoenicians did not have many vowel sounds in their language. The writing could be read without vowel letters.

The Phoenicians used their alphabet wherever they went. And soon other people began to use it, too.

Among the first people who used it were the Hebrews. They lived near Phoenicia.

The Old Testament of the Bible was first written down in this alphabet. The writing was done just as the Phoenician writing was done. It was put down from right to left. There were no vowel letters and no breaks at the ends of words or sentences.

אנכי יי אלהיך:

ארץ עשיתי ואדם

GOD THY LORD THE AM I

←

MAN AND EARTH CREATED I

Greece was another place where Phoenicians used their alphabet. The Greek people saw how useful the alphabet was and began to use it, too.

But they did not use the Phoenician alphabet just as it was. Their language had sounds that the Phoenician language did not have. And the Phoenician language had sounds that the Greeks did not have. So the Greeks changed the meaning of some letters and added two new ones.

Greek schoolboys 3,500 years ago wrote on papyrus, and on wax tablets. The tablets were flat pieces of wood with a small raised frame around the sides. A thin layer of wax was poured inside the frame and smoothed down. Letters were drawn in the wax with a sharp stick of metal or bone.

Important Greek writings were made on parchment. Parchment was a very thin sheet of leather. It was smooth to write on and lasted a long time. A pen made of a reed or a brush was used to write with.

The Etruscans who lived north of the Greeks saw many of these Greek writings and learned to use the alphabet, too. They made changes in it to suit their language just as the Greeks had done.

After the Etruscans borrowed the alphabet, they began to trade with the Romans. The Romans lived in the country we now call Italy. Rome was their main city.

The Romans saw how easily the Etruscans could write down their ideas. So before long the Romans, too, adopted the idea of writing with letters.

The Romans did not need certain letters that the Etruscans had in their alphabet. So they left these letters out, and added one letter that they did need. The Roman alphabet had twenty-three letters, three letters less than our alphabet.

The Romans changed the way most of the letters looked. The Greek alphabet and the Etruscan alphabet still had letters that looked like some of the hieroglyphic or cuneiform symbols. These letters were hard to make, and slowly people changed them. The new Roman letters were easy to make and looked much nicer. The final Roman alphabet looked like our alphabet of capital letters looks today. But even though the Romans changed the way the letters looked, they did not think of adding small letters.

HIERO-GLYPHIC	HIERATIC		PHOENI-CIAN	GREEK	ROMAN	
		A			A	
		G				C G
		D			D	
		H·E			E	
		F			F	
		CH			H	
		TH				
		E,Y			I	
		K			K	
		L			L	
		M			M	
		N			N	
		S				
		O			O	
		P			P	
		TS			R	
		K			S	
		R			T	
		SH			V	Y
		T			Q	
					X	
					Z	

The chart on the opposite page shows how the alphabet changed from the early Egyptian writing to the Roman alphabet.

On this chart you can also see what sounds the letters stood for in each of the different kinds of writing.

The Greeks did not need as many letters for consonants as the Phoenicians had. But the Greek language could not be written without letters for vowel sounds. So the Greeks made some of the Phoenician consonant letters stand for vowel sounds. And they added two more letters to complete the number of vowel letters they needed.

The Romans did not need letters for *th* and *ks* that the Etruscans had in their alphabet. So they dropped these two letters and added the letter *y*.

The Romans ruled over many other countries. They ruled Egypt, Phoenicia, Palestine, and Greece. They also ruled England, France, Spain, and Germany.

Wherever they ruled, the Romans used their alphabet. And people in those countries eventually used it, too. But most of the people in the conquered countries could not read and write.

The Roman soldiers who conquered other countries often brought some of the people of those countries back with them. These people were made to work without pay for people in Rome. They were slaves.

When slaves could read and write, they often became teachers for Roman boys. Only boys from rich Roman families learned to read and write.

ROME

ROMAN
EMPIRE
117 A.D.

Romans carved their letters on stone walls and wrote on parchment, papyrus, and wax tablets. During Roman days, too, paper was invented. Roman soldiers saw it in other countries and brought some to Rome. After that paper was used to write on.

Some Roman people wrote books, and many Romans read books written by Romans or by Greeks. These books were all written by hand on long sheets of paper or parchment. The sheets were rolled up into long scrolls and unwound when they were read.

Although many books and letters were written, most people could not read or write. People who could not read or write had necessary writing done for them by men called scribes. Scribes wrote messages for anyone who paid to have writing done.

After many years the Romans no longer ruled over the many countries around them. But the Roman alphabet was still used in those countries.

Some countries made small changes to suit themselves and their languages, just as changes had been made before. But on the whole, the alphabet did not change too much from the Roman alphabet in any country where it was used.

Our alphabet, the English alphabet, is the Roman alphabet with the letters *W*, *U*, and *J* added.

U and *W* came from the letter *V* about one thousand years ago. At first the letter *V* was used for all three sounds. But as new words using these sounds began to come into the language, the two new letters were needed.

They help to make the meaning of the writing clear.

The letter *J* came from the letter *I* about five hundred years ago. It, too, was needed to make the meaning of writing clear.

With the addition of these three letters, the English alphabet had the twenty-six letters we know.

The early English alphabet was written just like the Roman alphabet. It had only capital letters. There were no small letters. And all of the letters were printed.

Copies of early English books were made by hand just as copies of books had always been made. Most of the copying was done by men who spent their whole lives copying books. Sometimes it took one man a whole lifetime to copy one book.

It took less time to copy out a book after small letters were developed. And then when men began to run the small letters of each word together, as we do in handwriting, it took even less time. But still there were very few books. Even one page of a book cost too much for most people to buy. And because people could not get books to read, very few people had a chance to learn to read and write.

It was not until after 1450 that many people could buy books. In that year a man who lived in Germany, Johann Gutenberg, invented the printing press. After that books could be made in a short time, and they became less expensive. Only then, could many people have books and only then did many people learn how to read and write.

A is for *Apple* because long, long ago someone drew a picture and then someone made a pictogram, an ideogram, a phonogram, a syllabary, and finally a letter. You can learn to read and write *Apple* because we have letters for tools to learn with. The printing press makes our books so easily that now everyone can have many books for learning and for pleasure.